Contents

Acknowledgements

Thanks to Russ Towns at Windsports School, Holme Pierrepoint National Water Sports Centre and the Notts County Sailing Club, Hoveringham, for their help with the photographs, and to Jeremy Bays for the line illustrations.

1970s and early 80s. Since then most developments in the sport have been to do with equipment and the schooling system.

There is no age barrier to enjoying the sport; anyone from 8 to 80 (and more) can take part. However, the majority of windsurfers are in the 16–45 age group. While strength and fitness are helpful, they are by no means essential, but being able to swim is highly advisable.

Windsurfing essentially involves balancing the body against the wind, and good technique is vital.

Note Throughout the book sailors are referred to individually as 'he'. This should, of course, be taken to mean 'he or she' where appropriate.

Where to sail

In the United Kingdom the best place to start windsurfing is at a Royal Yachting Association (RYA) recognised centre. Alternatively, you can experiment for yourself in light winds on a small lake or gravel pit. Inland lakes are often privately owned and so, if sailing is allowed, payment is normally required.

Sailing clubs are often established on inland waters, but while most of them accept windsurfers, there are still some old-fashioned clubs who have yet to catch up with the times. Many of the clubs that do accept windsurfers offer launching facilities or day tickets. Fortunately, more and more specialist windsurfing clubs are now springing up.

Of course, the sea is free (except for parking!). However, currents, tides, strong winds and the absence of guaranteed rescue make the sea a place to avoid for the inexperienced. It is essential to seek local advice on access and conditions before launching at an unfamiliar location.

The RYA have up-to-date lists of cen-

(*Left to right*) Two types of wetsuit: a steamer and a summer suit

tres, clubs and venues, and local shops will also provide information and advice on places to sail.

Clothing

Windsurfers (except in very warm climates near the Equator) require protection against the cold because of the temperature of the water and, more importantly, the wind chill. Hypothermia can kill. You can always cool down if you are too hot by jumping in the water. However, if you get cold you will lose concentration and balance (meaning you fall off more), which can prove very dangerous.

Wetsuits

In the UK the water temperature makes the wearing of a wetsuit essential throughout the year. A wet suit should fit tightly, without constricting you, so as to reduce water flow through the suit to a minimum. There should be space around the arm muscles because tightness here causes you to tire early as your muscles expand.

Among the alternatives to the conventional wetsuit are steamers, which

2

are made of thicker material and are blind stitched with sealed seams to prevent water leakage. Thinner suits are great for summer use. If you feel the cold a 4 mm thick suit with detachable arms will serve you from late spring through to summer and autumn. In addition, the newer, flexible, neoprene suits ensure a very close fit that helps to keep you warm. Semi-dry and drysuits are another, often more expensive, alternative to a wetsuit, but they are only really necessary for winter use.

There are a large variety of wetsuits on the market, from the shorter styles right up to the full length steamer. The more you pay, the more warmth and comfort you can expect, although you do sometimes pay for the fashion element. It is worth trying on a number of wetsuits, or even considering a made-to-measure suit, to ensure that you get a comfortable fit.

Traditionally, wetsuits of the long johns type worn with a top have been a favourite first-time compromise, but improvements in materials and design make the one-piece suit a more sensible choice for many. There are also short-sleeved, one-piece suits with arms that can be added on for colder days, and these make a sensible summer option.

Buoyancy aids

Buoyancy is an important consideration when choosing clothing. Children and adults should wear a buoyancy aid, especially when learning, and a British Standard approved type is the best option. An alternative is a 'float coat' which is specifically designed for windsurfing. Combined with the wetsuit's buoyancy these aids help keep your head above water without restricting movement. Remember, however, that these are only aids. Some sailing venues have their own requirements regarding personal buoyancy.

Harnesses

As you improve you will require a harness which hooks on to the boom via a rope, relieving the arms and allowing you to sail for much longer periods. When you buy a harness try on several, checking that they feel comfortable and do not apply too much pressure anywhere. It is worth trying a variety of makes and sizes, because sizing varies a great deal. Although harnesses often have some buoyancy a 'float coat' is a sensible addition.

Gloves, helmets and shoes

Finally, the extremities will need protection. Hands are almost impossible to keep warm in cold conditions; gloves give some protection, but only at the expense of a loss of feel for the boom. Neoprene helmets are essential in the winter as a large proportion (25 per cent) of heat is lost from the head. Good footwear is also important. You can use plimsolls or training shoes to start with, as these provide grip and protection for the feet. Modern wetsuit boots grip well, which helps when learning, and good quality varieties will keep you warm and protect your feet.

Learning

The RYA is the governing body for the sport of windsurfing in the UK. Their learning scheme is split into units which build up to 5 separate levels, allowing you to learn at your own pace. Level 1 teaches you to sail wherever you wish in light winds, level 2 improves technique and the other levels deal with higher winds and, ultimately, shorter boards. The RYA have also introduced a junior scheme aimed at the 8 to 14-year-old group. This scheme uses recommended boards (about 320 cm in length with a daggerboard), which are easier for children to learn with. The teaching method starts the children on the water early, allowing them to enjoy themselves while gradually building up to a senior level 1 certificate.

While it is possible to teach yourself, this will take more time and will be a good deal more frustrating. Also you may pick up bad habits, inhibiting further progress. Learning at a RYA centre enables you to get on and enjoy the sport more quickly.

Types of board

There are a number of different types of board available and many windsurfers sail both long and short boards. Windsurfing boards have developed a great deal from the original heavy, flexible polyethylene boards of the late 1970s. The simplest way to define the different types of windsurfing board is by length, although in reality volume, underwater shape and to some extent materials have as much effect on performance. Generally, the more exotic and light the materials, the greater the cost, the rigidity and also the fragility of the board. Greater rigidity almost certainly helps performance, but you need to be good enough to turn that extra performance to advantage. A polyethylene board is a good first buy and is much more resilient to knocks than other materials.

When buying a board, seek advice from a reputable dealer; it should be in his interest to supply you with the right board and rig, but you must be honest about your requirements.

Weight/volume

The relationship between bodyweight and the volume of the board is demonstrated in fig. 1. To begin with you should have 150 to 160 litres more volume than your weight in kilograms to aid with learning. As you get better less volume is required for recreational sailing, especially in high winds.

As the graph shows, the lighter you are the smaller the board you need. This is why volume is so important, and it makes sense to move down in hull volume and size, especially for women and children. Smaller boards are easier to manoeuvre and control provided there is sufficient volume and stability. Always try out a board before purchasing it to see if the volume and size are correct; some manufacturers don't quite seem to get the volume right.

Most windsurfers start on a long school board, then move down to a 3.5 m length hull which enables them to sail in higher winds because of its lower volume. The underwater shape is not a critical factor when learning, but stability and a rounded tail will speed things up.

Long boards

Long boards with more flotation are best for light to moderate winds. The long boards measure between 3.5 and 3.8 m in length. They are good for learning but become difficult to control as the wind gets stronger. They have plenty of volume and stability. Race-boards are also available in this length range, and are suitable for more competent windsurfers.

Short boards

Short boards allow more control in higher winds, and they are also faster and more manoeuvrable. However, there is a catch with the smaller boards; they are harder to sail and so should be avoided until the basic skills have been mastered.

Those who wish to progress to strong-wind sailing will generally move on to shorter boards, but many windsurfers are content to stick with longer boards in all conditions.

A first short board requires more volume (about 120 to 150 litres), but again your size and weight will have an effect, and the key to your choice of board is that you must be able to uphaul it easily (i.e. stand and pull the sail up), or you will find learning hard, especially in the fickle British winds.

If you are looking to enjoy the waves and blast around at great speed, you will eventually move on to a sinker. A sinker has insufficient buoyancy to float with both a rig and a person on board. To sail a sinker, you start by lying in the water and letting the rig pull you out.

Race-boards

Another option is to continue sailing a long board and possibly start racing. There are several racing classes and disciplines. The race-board class (with rules based on production boards) is divided into 6 and 7.5 m² sail sizes.

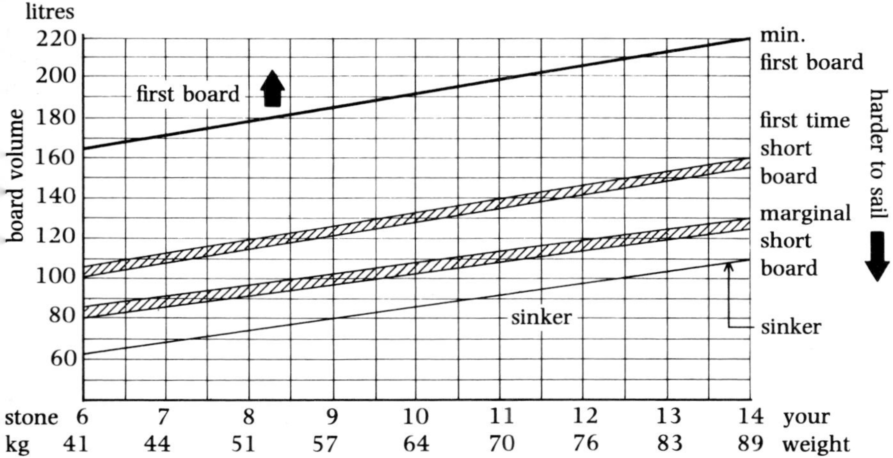

◀ Fig. 1   Weight/volume graph based on a RYA formula

5

Sails

Sail design has developed quite quickly in recent years. The early sails were floppy and unstable, which made them hard to control as the wind increased,

These days sails are like a foil, that is stable and controllable. In addition, they are more powerful, allowing you to use a smaller sail to go just as fast.

The 'soft' sail

Normally the standard sail supplied with a beginner's board is a 'soft' sail which has short battens that do no rigidly control the sail but allow it to be depowered. This has the advantage o making the sail more forgiving and also cheaper, even if it is a little less stable and powerful. The battens should be fully tensioned to help provide stability

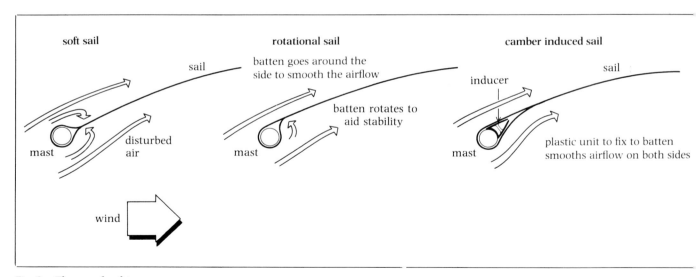

soft sail

sail

mast

disturbed air

wind

rotational sail

batten goes around the side to smooth the airflow

batten rotates to aid stability

mast

camber induced sail

sail

inducer

mast

plastic unit to fix to batten smooths airflow on both sides

Fig. 2   Theory of sail types

The rotational sail

As you improve it is worth considering a more stable and powerful 'rotational' sail. Some manufacturers now provide this sail as a standard rig package with the board. The rotational sail has battens the full width of the sail which flip round the mast and help to fix the sail's shape. The fact that the batten wraps around the mast means that the power from the sail comes on suddenly when you tack or gybe, and this is not easy to control initially. However, the extra power and control can be useful as you improve. Most short board sailors use this type of sail because it is light, powerful and yet stable. The rotational sail often costs more than the soft sail.

The 'camber induced' sail

The third type of sail is the 'camber induced' version. This sail has a piece of specially shaped plastic which fixes the batten very rigidly against the mast and holds it in position, controlling the shape and thereby creating more power. This type of sail is harder to uphaul because of the weight of water getting trapped in the wider luff sleeve.

Also, the sail can be very unforgiving; the power is either full on or off. Therefore, while this is not a sail to learn with, it is the ideal power source for the expert racer.

Some manufacturers are compromising on the theory behind this type of sail by using an external inducer to give the sail the stability and power of the camber-induced version as well as the lightness of the rotational variety.

Sail material

Sail material also comes into the cost equation. The vast majority of dinghy, cruiser and windsurfing sails are made of polyester, a woven, plastic fabric. A more expensive option is Mylar, which is a plastic film applied to the sail material to provide greater cloth stability. If it is treated well, Mylar contributes greatly to the sail's useful life because it helps prevent stretch, which is the eventual cause of the demise of many sails. Monofilm is a new, clear material which provides great stability for the sail. However, since it can be delicate and easy to scratch, it is mainly a material for the experts who want the ultimate in lightness and stability.

Sail size

The size of sail you will need depends on your experience, your weight and the wind strength. Children may initially use a sail measuring between 3 and 4 m² while adults often find a sail measuring between 5 and 6 m² a suitable first sail. Women and lightweight windsurfers will find smaller sails easier to manoeuvre and less powerful, thus helping to speed up the learning process.

The care and maintenance of sails

All sails last longer if they are washed, dried and rolled carefully in their sail bags. It is also sensible to release the battens and to repair any rips immediately. Don't leave the sail rigged on a rough surface such as tarmac, concrete or sand because the batten pockets and the sail itself can get scraped very easily. Also, remember that a sail should not be left flapping, as this also helps break up the material.

Parts of the board

The hull

The hull is the largest part of the board. The underside of the hull has a curve going from front to back along the centre line (known as the rocker) and smooth indentations underneath (known as the concaves). There are as many theories about hull design as there are board shapes, but there is little real difference between the larger manufacturers' hull shapes. It is more important to choose a design which is suited to your usage, size and expertise.

The hull should not be pulled over sand or gravel as this will scratch it.

Various types of material are used in manufacturing windsurfing hulls. Poly-ethylene is probably the best general purpose material, being tough, durable and fairly light. Moving up the cost scale we have ASA, which is a stiffer form of plastic. This is less popular nowadays and is less durable than polyethylene. It is often used as an outer skin to protect more exotic hulls. Finally, there are 'composites', which are normally epoxy resins reinforced with carbon or kevlar. While these are light and stiff, which helps performance, they are also expensive and fairly delicate.

The skeg

On the underside at the rear (or stern) of the board is the skeg, which provides directional stability. In high performance windsurfing the skeg is critical, providing both lift and control since at high speed it is the only part of the board that is in the water. Needless to say, better skegs normally cost more. The skeg supplied with the board should be quite adequate for general windsurfing.

The daggerboard

Longer boards also have a daggerboard to help prevent the board from sliding sideways. As the board goes faster the daggerboard becomes less important and it is then retracted into the hull; this is known as a fully retracting dagger-board. The retraction of the dag-gerboard is useful for sailing off wind (see p. 21), when the skeg comes into its own.

Daggerboards are normally made of plastic. They also give stability to the hull, which is useful when learning.

The deck

The top surface or deck is non-slip and often has footstraps. These straps are useful in stronger winds because they help you to control the board and stay in contact with the hull. However, they are more of a hindrance when learning, and so are best removed. The newer board designs have a domed (curved) deck at the rear to help with control and comfort.

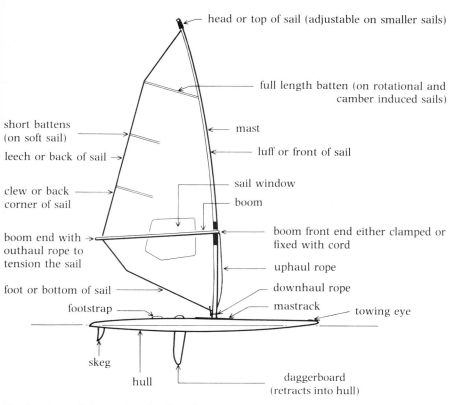

head or top of sail (adjustable on smaller sails)

full length batten (on rotational and camber induced sails)

short battens (on soft sail)

mast

luff or front of sail

leech or back of sail

sail window

clew or back corner of sail

boom

boom end with outhaul rope to tension the sail

boom front end either clamped or fixed with cord

uphaul rope

foot or bottom of sail

downhaul rope

footstrap

mastrack

towing eye

skeg

hull

daggerboard (retracts into hull)

Fig. 3   Parts of the windsurfing board

The mast

Many boards have a mastrack which allows the mast to slide forwards and backwards. This track enables the experts to achieve better balance and control over the board. When starting to sail put the mastrack in a central position.

The unit between the mastrack and the mast is known as the mastfoot, and this universal joint (UJ) holds the key to the windsurfing sailing system, allowing the mast and the rig to pivot in any direction in relation to the board for steering and control. The mastfoot connects the hull and the rig and is located just forward of the daggerboard.

The line between the mastfoot and the bottom of the sail is known as the downhaul. This tensions the sail along the front (or luff), which affects the stability and performance of the sail by determining the position of its fullness. The downhaul should be pulled tight on most sails for the best control.

Many boards also have a mast extension. This makes it possible to extend the mast length to fit a variety of sails.

The rig

The rig consists of a mast (the pole in the front or luff of the sail), the sail and the boom (the horizontal unit). The parts of the sail are shown in fig. 3, and it can be seen that the battens may either be full length or short.

Matching the mast with the sail is important. Finding the correct length gives better control and power and also makes rigging easier. Masts are made of epoxy, carbon fibre and aluminium, and the degree of stiffness and bend varies a great deal. Generally, stiffer masts are used for higher performance sails.

The mastrack. Note also the mast extension and the universal joint

The bow

The front of the board is known as the bow. All boards should have a towing eye inserted here for rescue purposes, and it is a good idea to fix a loop of cord through this eye, just in case you ever need towing. The towing eye can also act as a tie-down point to the front of a car.

Other fittings

All the adjustable fittings (such as booms etc.) should be cleaned thoroughly of sand after sailing or they will be liable to jam and become unusable.

A clamp on boom fitting ▶

Rigging

Sail rigging to perfection is an acquired art. You should seek the advice of your local windsurfing centre or shop on the correct sequence of rigging and setting the sail up, because this varies accord-

ing to type and manufacturer. The following is the basic method of rigging most sails.

Having unrolled the sail on a soft surface, slip it on to the mast and apply a little downhaul; this makes it easier to fit the boom. Next, attach the boom at approximately shoulder height, either with a rope system or with a clamp boom which uses cord, wire or plastic and a mechanical lever to solidly fix the boom to the mast. It is vital that the boom is rigid and tightly fixed to the mast because this helps with control of the rig. Care must be taken not to over-tighten the boom and crush the mast. Ask your instructor or a knowledgeable friend to help you with rigging while you are learning; a badly rigged sail is difficult to control.

The correct boom height can be obtained by standing the boom up and measuring the height against your shoulders, and then against the mast. Don't stand the mast up as this may clog the bottom with sand and soil. Use tape to mark the correct position for the boom on the mast.

The more traditional method of fixing uses a cleated rope wrapped around the

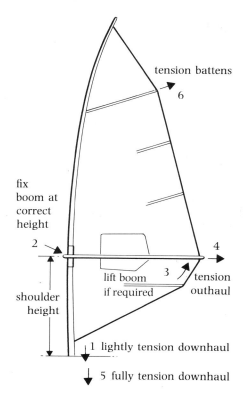

Fig. 4   Rigging a sail

Stage 1 of the rope system for connecting the boom to the mast. The boom is parallel to the mast and the rope is taken round before being tied off

Stage 2: the boom is raised to 90° to the mast and the rope is tightened to ensure a good fit

The recommended length of the boom will normally be printed on the sail, and it is sensible to check this with a tape measure. Many booms have spring-loaded pins which slot into holes to vary the length.

Finally, you should tension the battens (if they are the full length type) and retighten the downhaul to remove all horizontal creases. Also, raise the rig, making sure that it looks right and check the harness lines (if you are using them) on the shore, readjusting as necessary.

On a soft sail it is possible to reduce power and flatten the sail with more outhaul and downhaul, and this is probably the best way of rigging such a sail to begin with.

If you are leaving the rig unattended, tie it to something solid because a flying rig is very dangerous. To take the rig apart do the opposite of the above. After use, rinse the sail thoroughly in fresh water and make sure it is dry before rolling it up and storing it in its bag.

mast. The method has many permutations, but your dealer should be able to help you. The boom is fastened while parallel to the mast before being swung through 90° to a horizontal position where it is tightened. Many wavesailors (those who sail in waves and in surf) still use this method due to its reliability, but it is more difficult to learn.

The next stage involves threading and tensioning the outhaul, which is the cord at the outer end of the boom.

Lifting the board ▶

Getting to
the water

The board is a heavy object, and so it should be lifted with care to prevent back damage. Boards can generally be carried by the daggerboard case and steadied by the other hand on the mast step. Place the board near the water. Check that the daggerboard is in and that it rotates easily, and also check that the skeg is securely fixed.

Lifting the rig

Lifting the rig can be very awkward due to the pressure of the wind on the sail. Conversely, the rig can be as light as a feather if it is lifted correctly. The secret is to let the wind do the work. Stand with your back to the wind and lift the rig by the mast and the boom so that the wind gets underneath the sail. Walk with the rig this way (see photo above) and then put it in the water. Next, fetch the board and connect it up so that the rig is down wind and the bow or front is facing the direction in which you wish to go.

The first
steps afloat

At a RYA centre your first steps on a board will be on a windsurfing simulator on dry land. This enables the instructor to demonstrate the basic movements and techniques on a special unit. You can then practise and be corrected without getting wet, saving an enormous amount of time and energy. Once you are on the water it will soon become evident whether or not you have been listening and taking note during practice sessions.

The RYA centre has rescue facilities, which is important when you first start windsurfing as you often need fetching when you drift down wind. Getting your technique perfected early on really does pay dividends, making the RYA centre's fee a very worth while investment.

Should you decide to learn on your own or with a friend's help, make sure that there is someone watching in case you get into difficulty. Start on a small lake where you can get to shore easily; when learning it is dangerous to sail on the sea if the wind is blowing away from the shore. 'Offshore winds', as they are known, appear to be deceptively light and gentle on land, but once you are away from the shelter of the land they will double in strength, taking you further away from the shore and help. In addition, the waves will increase in size and you will get into difficulties, drifting further and further out to sea.

Uphauling. Make the approach from the opposite side to the rig with the wind coming from behind

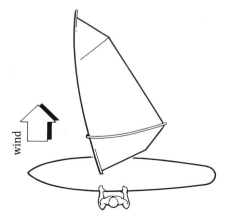

◄ Fig. 5   Rig and board placement

Launching

Begin by checking the wind direction by looking at the flags or waves. Check that the rig is placed down wind and that the daggerboard is fully down (this ensures that you are at least knee-deep in water). Stand on the opposite side to the rig and climb on to the board with your hands either side of the mast, keeping your weight over the centre line so that the board does not tip. Try walking around a little to get the feel of the board, then when you are more confident, uphaul the rig.

For this first lesson on the water many schools tether the boards by passing a cord through the dagger case to an anchor or buoy.

Uphauling can be the most tiring action when learning, and good technique is essential. Start by kneeling on the centre of the board and check that the wind is coming from behind. Grasp the uphaul for stability and stand up, positioning the feet either side of the mastfoot and also on the centre line. Bend the knees a little and use your

Pull the rig clear of the water, keeping the back straight and the knees bent

Work hand over hand to raise the rig

weight and the strength in your legs to pull the rig partially clear of the water; this is the difficult part because of the weight of water in the sail. Make sure that your legs rather than your back take the strain.

As the sail frees itself from the water it becomes easier to uphaul, and you should then work up the rope hand over hand. Grasp the mast with both hands just below the boom. Then try manoeuvring the board by leaning the rig

15

Incline the rig towards the front to turn the board away from the wind

Incline the rig towards the back to turn the board towards the wind

The secure position

towards the back and front of the board while holding the mast (leaning the rig towards the back makes the board turn into the wind). Return to the original position with the rig at right angles to the board. This is known as the **secure position**.

If the rig is upwind of the board when you start uphauling, you will need to raise the rig so that it is slightly clear of the water, then let the wind get under it and swing the board round. If you are not careful the rig will take you with it, and an involuntary swim will follow.

However, if the rig is now down wind you can uphaul it properly as above.

Often the first reaction when in the secure position is to pull on the boom and try to sail straight off; this generally results in a swim. Unless you start your session on the water by trying to turn

From the secure position identify a goal point

the board round, you may never be seen again! The best way to learn to turn is to lean the rig to the front or the back and shuffle the board round under your feet. Keeping the rig over the centre line is really just a matter of maintaining your balance and using the sail correctly.

Sailing away

Find a point to aim for on the opposite shore such as a tree or a bush. This should be ahead of you and at right angles to the direction of the wind, and is known as the **goal point**.

Release the mast with your back hand (the hand nearest the back of the board). Move your back foot over the daggerboard case, keeping it on the centre line. Move the front foot back to a position behind the mast step, and point it forwards so that you can keep your balance as the wind fills and pulls on the sail.

You will need to concentrate hard on the next stage. Turn to face the direction in which you are going, then pull the rig right across the body to a point at right angles to the board where it balances and feels light; this is known as the **balance point**. You can try this on dry land first by pulling the rig over and clapping your hands when it feels balanced; the rig should be where you left it if you have found the balance point.

The problem when you try and grab the rig too early is that the board starts steering upwind (towards the wind) and the sail loses power, which invariably results in a ducking. When the rig is at the balance point, rest your hand on the boom and pull it in so that the rig fills with wind, transferring your weight to the back foot at the same time. When you are ready (there is no rush) move your front hand to the boom. This is known as the **sailing position**.

Place the front hand on the mast step behind the mast and point the front foot forwards on the centre line with the back foot at 90°

17

Draw the rig across the body to the balance point

Aim to sail across the wind (at right angles) towards the goal point. You are now sailing on a reach, that is the direction you are going in relation to the wind (see fig. 7). If you are below or above the goal point you should steer to correct the course (see p. 19).

Place the back hand on the boom near to where your shoulder is at this point

The importance of learning to uphaul and start sailing correctly cannot be over-emphasised as it is crucial to windsurfing, allowing you to develop the correct stance and sail easily and comfortably. The stance you adopt is important both for stability and speed.

Pull in with the back hand and pivot the rig round to your side so that you can see the goal down the side of the mast

The head should be held up so that you can see where you are going. The arms should be slightly bent and shoulder-width apart, and the shoulders should be parallel to the boom. The back should be straight and the bottom tucked in.

When the board has picked up speed and you are comfortable, transfer your front hand on to the boom either where your front shoulder now is or 15 cm (6 in) away from the front of the boom

The front leg should be straight and the back leg slightly bent so that you can control the power. The feet should be approximately shoulder-width apart.

Steering

Imagine you are pushing the board from the side: it will almost certainly pivot about the daggerboard and turn one way or the other. However, if the board is balanced it will just go sideways, and this position represents **the centre of lateral resistance**.

Another way of thinking about this is to compare it to a revolving door pivoting around a point (the centre of lateral resistance): push to the left and the door turns that way; push to the right and it goes the other way.

Windsurfing is about balancing forces, so that when the rig's force is balanced over the centre of lateral resistance, the board travels in a straight line. Steering makes use of this fact. If you push the rig forward with the sail filled, the force or power from the rig will be forward of this central balance point, thus pushing the front round away from the wind (known as bearing away). Moving the rig backwards means that the back is pushed round and the front turns up towards the

wind; this is known as **luffing**, and it allows the windsurfer to steer in any direction.

At a windsurfing centre you will try out this section of the learning process on a simulator before going on to the water. The movements have to be fairly exaggerated on a long board.

The power of the sail is quite simply controlled by using the back hand as the throttle. Pushing this hand out moves the boom out at the back and reduces the power in the sail. Sheeting or pulling in the hand until the sail stops flapping and feels the most powerful, means that you have maximum power. As the wind increases, use your bodyweight to counterbalance this greater power by leaning out. You will only be able to cope with a certain amount of power, and as the wind increases you will require a smaller sail. The amount of power you can handle (and the sail size you choose) depends on your technique and size.

When first sheeting in there are several common mistakes to be aware of. You may not allow sufficiently for the power, resulting in your being pulled forward over the front. If there is too

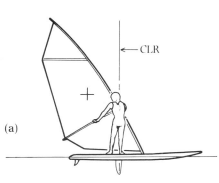

(a)

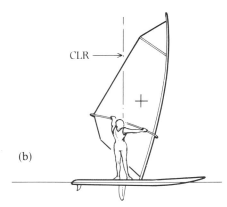

(b)

sail's force balanced

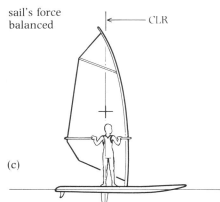

(c)

Fig.6 Steering

(a) Sail's force is behind the board's centre of lateral resistance (CLR) so the board turns up in to the wind

(b) Sail's force is forward of CLR so the board turns away from the wind

(c) Sail's force is balanced

little commitment when sheeting in, the front of the sail is unfilled (it may flap a little) and then the board turns into wind because of the force of the sail. This means that the sail 'backs', throwing you in the water backwards due to the reduced force being generated by the empty sail. Practise to learn the correct technique.

▲ Incline the rig towards the back of the board to turn the front of the board upwind of your goal

◄ Incline the rig to the front to steer the board down wind of your goal

Aerodynamic theory

It is important to learn to make use of the flow of the wind over the sail to propel the board forward. The sail has a shape like the aerodynamic foil of one side of an aeroplane wing which creates a pull in both a forward and sideways direction, so that the closer to the wind or the slower you are travelling, the more sideways force is exerted. This sideways force is resisted by the skeg and the daggerboard, allowing the board to go straight ahead. When the wind is coming from the side or behind the force has more of a forward component. As a result, when a board is sailing fast offwind it only requires a skeg at the back to resist the sideways force of the sail to keep it on course. As the board goes faster it rises on top of the water and skims the surface, creating much less resistance; this is known as **planing**.

Judging the wind

When you start sailing you reach across the wind, which is at 90° to the board. Then when you turn the board round you will probably drift down with the wind, and to get back to where you started you will need to steer upwind (by putting the rig towards the back of the board). You will soon find that there is a limit as to how close to the wind the board will go before the sail starts to flap. If this happens, you will need to turn the board away from the wind to avoid falling in. Balancing the rig so that you are as close as possible to the wind is known as being **close hauled** (see fig. 7). When the sail is flapping you are in the **no go zone**.

To get back upwind you have to sail in one direction, again as close as possible to the wind, then turn round and proceed in the opposite direction, again as close as possible to the direction of the wind (see the dotted lines in fig. 7). This is known as **tacking**. Long boards with daggerboards are much more efficient at this, especially in lighter winds. In addition to the daggerboard, specialist racing boards use the edges or rails of the board to help grip the water, and this enables them to achieve maximum upwind performance.

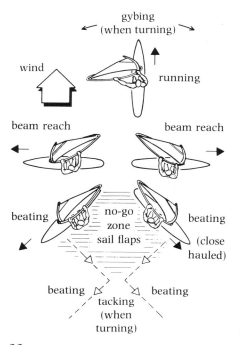

◀ Fig. 7   Points of sailing

Running

Running is the point of sailing where the wind comes from directly behind. In this instance there is no sideways pull to balance against and also no aerodynamic lift, making it the most difficult point of sailing. The problem is to do with stability, and a good sense of balance is necessary. The daggerboard will help with stability but as the wind increases it may start to hinder progress as it tends to tip you up. This is due to the lift that is produced by going through the water and when this happens the daggerboard should be retracted.

Tacking

Tacking or turning the front of the board through the wind and the no go zone is achieved quite simply by moving the rig towards the back of the board. This allows you to get the front directly into the wind and beyond, which is known as **head to wind**. As you reach

this point, transfer your front hand to the mast and shuffle the board round slowly as when turning. Resume the secure position then sail off as previously described. As you get better this becomes one continuous smooth movement, and the board is kept moving through head to wind. Eventually the secure position is missed out; proficient sailors throw the rig round and hardly lose speed when turning.

Turning through 180°. Incline the rig to the rear, taking small steps around the mastfoot and keeping your feet near the centre line ▼

Gybing

Gybing is a manoeuvre you may unwittingly do while turning through 180°. It essentially involves turning the front of the board away from the wind on to a run (see fig. 7), when the wind comes from directly behind, and turning back on to a reach while the sail crosses the front of the board. On a short board this is the quickest way to turn. Gybing can be difficult to start with due to the sudden pull that is felt from the sail when you turn on to the new direction.

To gybe incline the rig forwards towards the front of the board, keeping the sail filled, and turn the board away from the wind (as described in the section on steering). To begin with you can shuffle the sail round holding the mast, as in tacking. As you become more proficient you can use the rig to propel you round further until you hardly use the mast. In addition, as you improve you can use your weight to steer the board by depressing the hull on one side.

Stopping

Quite simply all you have to do to stop is to release the 'throttle' or your back hand from the boom and then grasp the mast. If you need to stop any faster, lay the rig on the water; the propulsion is then lost and you come to a stop. However, do make sure that there is no one nearby who could be hit by your mast or sail.

You can also control the speed by letting out the back hand, which takes the power out of the sail. As you become more proficient you will be able to sail to shore, depower the rig and simply step off, which looks very impressive.

Always approach the shore slowly so as not to damage your equipment or other people. Once on the shore, lay the rig down wind so that it doesn't get blown away. Then put your board on top to weight the rig down.

Harnesses

When you start sailing in stronger winds your arms will tire easily. Many windsurfers, however, seem to spend hours on end on the water and still come in looking fresh. The reason they can do this is because they have been wearing a harness with a hook which connects to lines on the boom and takes the strain off the arms. This is why windsurfing is accessible to so many people of different sizes. The harness makes longer windsurfing sessions not only feasible but highly enjoyable, placing the emphasis on good technique rather than brute strength.

You should be proficient at sailing in moderate winds before attempting to use a harness. There are three types of harness generally available.

1. The **seat harness** is probably the most popular. It looks like a nappy and using by a low hook position it allows you to control more sail area and transfer power to the strongest muscles in your legs. The seat harness comes with

a limited amount of buoyancy and there are several hook heights for different disciplines. The lower hook positions tend to be for specialist speed and racing sailors since they are more difficult to learn with. However, once mastered the low hook position is often considered best for general sailing.

2. The original harness design is the **chest or shoulder harness**. Although the high hook position is favoured by wavesailors, many find it gives them less back support. Also, the higher hook

(*Left*) A seat harness. (*Right*) A chest harness

Setting up harness lines

position means less power can be transmitted from the rig to the hull.

3. The **waist harness** has similar properties to the chest harness except that it has a lower hook position, and so pulls from the lower back. Again, many wavesailors favour the ease of hooking and unhooking. The lines need to be longer than for the chest harness, making it a little more difficult to use.

All harnesses should have a 'V' safety hook to help prevent rope tangle.

A harness is relatively easy to use when you are fairly confident on a board in a good breeze. The harness lines should be attached to the boom shoulder-width apart. The line length can be determined in relation to the distance between your clenched fist and your elbow. The key to setting the lines is to match their centre point to the centre of pull from the sail. You do this by holding the sail correctly (on shore), and then moving both hands to a central point. The harness lines should be the same distance either side of this point and they will then balance the pull from the rig and be easy to use. The lines should be of the correct stiffness; if they are too floppy they will tangle, while if they are too stiff you won't be able to hook in to them.

Hooking in to the lines is simply a matter of flicking the lines into the hook by pulling the rig towards you, and leaning back when the line slips in the hook. Unhooking is simply a matter of pulling the rig towards you so that the lines drop out. If there is more pull from either the left or the right arm, you must move the line position in order to compensate for this and balance the rig again. Hooking and unhooking can be practised ashore.

Safety considerations

There are several safety considerations, all of which are a matter of common sense.

1. Never go out on your own, and make sure friends know where you are. In addition, keep your eye on companions wherever you sail.

2. Observe the 'rules of the road' (see p. 27). Keep well clear of commercial craft; they move surprisingly fast and cannot manoeuvre very easily, especially in harbours where they have to keep to channels.

3. Consult all the available forecasts on the television, the radio and in the newspapers; in the UK the BBC and ITV put out forecasts after the news, and Radio 4 broadcasts shipping forecasts. Another useful source of information is the RYA booklet (G5), which has times and explanations of the forecasts. Also, remember that the sky can give good warning of weather changes; for example dark clouds, especially in

Self-rescue. By dragging the boom in the water you can drift towards the shore

In light winds and for a short distance you could lay the rig across the back of the board and paddle home

summer, can mean a change for the worse.

4. Avoid offshore winds (see p. 14).
5. Carry some spare line with you for emergency repairs.
6. Avoid areas with strong tides, and keep ashore when visibility is poor. You can tell that there is a tide if water is swirling around a buoy or post. Tides can sweep you away, and they are most dangerous half-way between low and high water when the currents are strongest.
7. Finally, and perhaps most obviously, don't go out in conditions you are unable to handle; that is just being foolish.

Self-rescue

Even though, hopefully, you will never require them, you should learn the skills required for self-rescue. The first and golden rule is always to stay with the board, since it floats and is fairly visible. If you can't get ashore, roll the sail up. You should always tie a safety leash between the rig and board, because if the rig comes loose the board can blow away faster than you can swim, and your life could be in jeopardy if the shore is any great distance away.

Forty-five minutes is the longest time recommended for sailing without a rest in fresh winds. Don't stay out very long if conditions are deteriorating; you will tire more easily and then things can get worse very quickly.

There are several methods of getting back to shore. If the shore is at right angles to the wind and the board is pointing towards the shore, half-lift the sail, leaving the end of the boom in the water; you will then drift fairly rapidly to safety. Alternatively, you could lay the rig across the back of the board and paddle back or put the rig on the board, climb inside the boom and paddle back with the mast facing into the wind.

Finally, you can roll the rig and paddle back. To do this you have to remove the battens and disconnect the boom at both the outer and then the inner end, laying it along the mast. Roll the rig, tie it at either end and lay it down the board. Next, you simply lie on top and paddle home. This sounds easy but requires practise on a windless day on a local lake.

Getting help

There are several things you can do if you are unable to get ashore and need to summon help. Flares are useful on large stretches of water and the sea, and there are some small, waterproof types

available. These are easy to carry round your waist in a ski or 'bum bag'. A dayglo flag (available from the RYA) is also a very useful way of attracting attention and it is sensible to carry one wherever you sail. The International Distress Signal involves raising your hands above your head and then bringing them down in a waving motion (with clenched fist). A whistle can also be useful.

Insurance

A windsurfing board and rig can be lethal, not only on the water but if it comes off a car or if the rig or board fly away on shore. Therefore third party insurance is a cheap and very sensible precaution. Most inland lakes require proof of insurance before allowing you to sail. There are specialist brokers you can go to (who advertise in Windsurfing magazines), and they will also insure your equipment against theft (provided that it is secured).

When on shore you should always secure your rig and board to something solid; even in light winds it can blow away and hurt someone.

'Rules of the road'

Right of way rules are just as important on the water as they are on the public road. They can be summarised very simply.

1. Powered craft should keep clear of boards except in confined waters: ships or ferries within or near a harbour are often unable to keep clear and may not have seen a small windsurfer. Large boats can't manoeuvre easily and often take miles to slow down. Anyway, common sense dictates that they are very much bigger than you!
2. When two sailing craft are approaching each other the one with the wind coming from the starboard has right of way. If you are on the starboard tack the wind will be coming over the right-hand side of your board. The simplest way to work this out is to see if your right hand is the front one. If your left hand is forward you generally do not have the right of way.
3. If two sailing craft are on the same tack, then the one closest to the wind

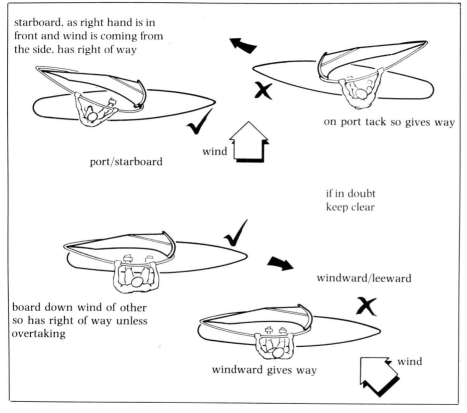

starboard, as right hand is in front and wind is coming from the side, has right of way

port/starboard

on port tack so gives way

wind

if in doubt
keep clear

board down wind of other so has right of way unless overtaking

windward/leeward

windward gives way

wind

has to give way. The same applies for a board or a boat that is overtaking.

Make sure that when you change course you do it deliberately. If you are on a collision course with another craft you should always pass port to port (or left to left); that way you don't turn into each other. Further details are available in the International Regulations for Preventing Collisions at Sea (RYA booklet G2). These basic rules form the basis of the racing rules.

Sometimes in high surf different rules apply due to the extreme conditions.

Always remember to use your common sense and keep clear of other water-users.

◀ Fig. 8   Basic right of way rules

Transportation

Most sailors take their boards home after sailing because of the possibility of theft. While a board is easy to transport if you have a car, it is also necessary to have a strong bar type roof-rack or a tow bar and trailer. The roof-rack should be able to carry weights up to the manufacturer's maximum recommendation for the car; this is usually between 60–75 kg. The uplift of the board when travelling is considerable so it should always be placed nose-down and pointing forwards.

Tying a line from the towing eye at the front of the board to the towing hook under the car is a sensible precaution, and is sometimes required for the insurance. Remember to protect the bonnet paintwork of your car, as a vibrating cord can do a lot of damage. The boom can either be taken to bits and put inside the car or placed on the top of the board (with padding).

Sails should be carried rolled up and then laid flat inside the car. If you must carry them on the roof, always bag them up or use a sail tube. A padded roof-rack cover will also help protect the board.

The mast should be secured alongside the board. It can be dangerous when the car is stationary, so tie something bright to the end. If it overhangs by more than a metre it must have something to mark the end by law and if it overhangs by more than 1.8 m you will need special boards.

Finally, make sure that everything is securely tied down. It is illegal to travel with a dangerous load which is a hazard to other road-users. Rubber bungie cords with hooks on the end should never be used as they are not designed for the sort of force a windsurfer puts on them. The correct roof-rack straps are available from windsurfing dealers and cost very little. You can also buy special kits with supports, mast holders and the like, should you wish.

Taking things further

The joy of windsurfing is that it gives you the freedom to take the sport to your own personal limit. Most windsurfers progress to cruising on either long or short boards. However, no one has yet approached the limits of the sport, and even world champions are still learning new techniques and tricks.

Racing is a popular facet of the sport. It is a superb way to improve your skills and meet sailors of a like mind. Most racing takes place on long boards. The two internationally recognised classes are 6 and 7.5 m². The 6 m² class has a fairly loose set of rules. The hulls are biased towards light wind sailing, and the smaller rigs favour lightweight sailors.

The flatter race boards of the 7.5 m² class perform best when the wind is over 11 knots and they are planing. In addition there are specialist boards such as the Olympic board, with a rounded hull design. Finally, on the professional circuit there are custom boards similar to production race-boards but lighter and stiffer. The Mistral and Windsurfer classes race on identical boards and rigs.

There are two racing organisations in the UK. The United Kingdom Boardsailing Association (UKBSA) uses the same International Racing Rules as are used in yachting (with some amendments), and sail in winds over 5 knots. The alternative is the higher wind racing of

Gybing around a mark during a course race

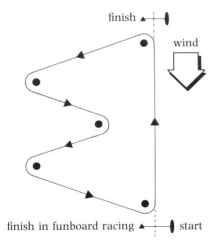

Fig.9   A course race or 'M' course

the British Windsurfing Association (BWA), who only sail when the wind speed is over 11 knots, by which time the modern race-board tends to plane. The BWA set their courses with the emphasis on fast reaching. However, the 11-knot wind limit often means there is little racing at some events due to lack of wind. Both types of racing are fun and well supported at national level.

To start racing, join a local club race, then move on to regional and national competitions.

Course racing

Course racing is a discipline which involves sailing a short distance upwind, reaching down wind round a long course, and then going back up again. A short board is used in high winds and a long race-board in lesser winds. This is probably the most popular form of racing.

Freestyle

This involves 'playing' on a long board that is learning how it handles and

This sailor demonstrates a 'railride' in a freestyle contest

Speed sailing

responds by doing tricks and demonstrating balance and handling skills. Freestyle is a great summer activity, allowing you to keep fit and get plenty of practice.

The most popular trick is railriding, which consists of sailing a board on its edge. There are also fancy ways of tacking and gybing, all of which can make up an extensive repertoire. There are a number of detailed books on this subject.

Speed sailing

The world speed record for windsurfing is 72 k.p.h. (45 m.p.h.). Speed boards are thin, long, specialist boards which are difficult to sail. Speed is something we can all enjoy and relate to, making speed sailing the ultimate goal for many sailors.

Slalom

BWA events include slalom which is a fast and furious form of racing on a down wind or figure-of-eight reaching

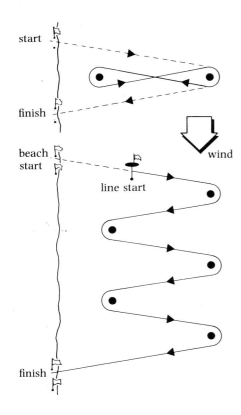

course, with several buoys close to the beach. It is a great spectator sport in strong winds, involving skill in board control and handling.

Wavesailing

Wavesailing consists of both sailing in to the shore on the waves and jumping on the way out from the shore. Wavesailing is a popular 'cruising' pastime. Learning to control a board coming in on the waves is known as **waveriding**; changing direction is known as **transitions**. On the way out to sea **jumping**, as the name implies, consists of getting the board airborne. The experts can even loop boards in the air in a complete circle, and watching them is highly entertaining. Wavesailing is the section of the sport to which many sailors aspire because of its spectacular nature.

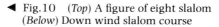

◀ Fig.10 (*Top*) A figure of eight slalom (*Below*) Down wind slalom course

Wavesailing